Clark Public Library
303 Westfield Ave.
Clark, NJ 07066
(732)388-5999

DIGITAL AND INFORMATION LITERACY ™

GOOGLE AND YOU

MAXIMIZING YOUR GOOGLE EXPERIENCE

PHILIP WOLNY

rosen publishing's
rosen central®

New York

For Jonatan Kaye

Published in 2012 by The Rosen Publishing Group, Inc.
29 East 21st Street, New York, NY 10010

Library of Congress Cataloging-in-Publication Data

Wolny, Philip.
Google and you: maximizing your Google experience/Philip Wolny. — 1st ed.
    p. cm. — (Digital and information literacy)
Includes bibliographical references and index.
ISBN 978-1-4488-5553-7 (lib. bdg.)—
ISBN 978-1-4488-5613-8 (pbk.)—
ISBN 978-1-4488-5614-5 (6-pack)
1. Google—Juvenile literature. I. Title.
ZA4234.G64W65 2012
025.042'52—dc23

                                                                    2011021215

Manufactured in the United States of America

CPSIA Compliance Information: Batch #W12YA: For further information, contact Rosen Publishing, New York, New York, at 1-800-237-9932.

CONTENTS

INTRODUCTION

A huge and ever-growing repository of instantly available information lies at our fingertips. Most readers are familiar with search engines. The most famous of them, Google, is one of the most visited Web sites in the world. Thanks to the Internet and the machines that allow us to surf it, we are getting more high-speed information whenever and wherever we want it.

Google, Inc., the pioneering Internet and technology company, has utterly revolutionized the way most of us live. While it was not the first search engine—it followed the likes of Go, Lycos, and Yahoo!—it has become so much a part of our daily activities that "Google" has become a verb. Whenever we need to look up information, we say, "I'll Google that." For many people, Google is now synonymous with "to search." Chances are you Google something, or use one of Google, Inc.'s other Web-based services, at least once every day, if not frequently throughout the day.

In this book, we will explore Google's search engine and demonstrate how to maximize your use of it and other Google services and offerings. Google allows you to do it all—from looking something up, to reading important documents online, to creating your own projects and content with services like Google Docs, for example. You can harness Google's valuable resources to create lively and in-depth multimedia projects, compose

Though not the only search engine available to Internet users, Google is the leader by far. It often seems like everyone in the world, every day, is "Googling."

thoroughly researched and content-rich reports, satisfy your curiosity about the world and its places and people, pursue your interests, and perform everyday tasks quickly and easily.

We will also review how to surf the Internet responsibly and use any information gathered in a proper and legal fashion. We will discuss how to be a good "citizen" of the online community, and how to balance a growing dependence on Google and other Internet services with continuing to live in the real world and experience its riches firsthand. So let's get online and explore the fascinating world of Google and you!

Chapter 1

Getting Started with Google

With the Internet constantly expanding, the amount of information to search through increases daily. Whether you are looking for information on a specific person, place, product, or subject, the more general the search term you use, the greater the number of results you will be presented with by Google. Looking up the word "store," for instance, yields almost three billion results. This is far too large a collection of Web sites to wade through. Typing in "sporting goods store," however, plus your local ZIP code, will narrow down the results tremendously.

Using more search terms in this manner allows Google to find more specific and useful results. In the following pages, we will take a look at some ways of narrowing down your search terms and generating more tightly focused and useful results.

Searching for Exact Words and Phrases

One way to narrow a search is to look for an exact phrase. If you're looking for information on the U.S. Constitution, you can simply plug in the words

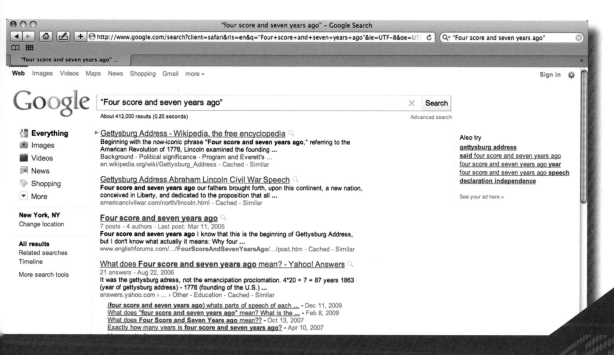

Google's results page for the opening lines of President Abraham Lincoln's famous Gettysburg Address are shown here (http://www.google.com). Note how the user typed the speech's opening phrase into the search box with quotes around it to receive relevant results that included exactly that phrase.

"we the people," without the quotations, and Google will usually search first for that exact phrase, since it is so well known. But after the initial results, you may start to see Web sites listed that simply contain any of those three words somewhere within the sites' text.

Putting your search terms in quotes will yield only the sites in which those words—"we the people"—appear in the exact order in which you typed them. For instance, if you were having trouble remembering who began his famous speech with "Four score and seven years ago," you could look up that phrase and confirm that it derives from President Abraham Lincoln's Gettysburg Address. For even more specific and tightly focused searches, you can use combinations of two or more phrases, written in separate sets of quotation marks.

File   Edit   View   Favorites   Tools   Help

QUICK SEARCH TIPS

Quick Search Tips

Some Google quick tips to refine your searches:

- Synonym search: If you want to search not only for your search term but also for its synonyms, place the tilde sign (~) immediately in front of your search term.
- To see a definition for a word or phrase, simply type the word "define," then a space, then the word(s) you want defined. To see a list of different definitions from various online sources, you can type "define:" followed by a word or phrase.
- Spell checker: Google's spell checking software automatically checks whether your query uses the most common spelling of a given word. If it thinks you're likely to generate better results with an alternative spelling, it will ask, "Did you mean: (more common spelling)?" Click the suggested spelling to launch a Google search for that term.
- Plus operator: Google ignores common words and characters such as "where," "the," "how," and other digits and letters that slow down your search without improving the results. If a common word is essential to getting the results you want, you can draw attention to it by putting a "+" sign in front of it.
- Related search: To search for Web pages that have similar content to a given site, type "related:" followed by the Web site address into the Google search box.
- Fill in the blank: Get Google to "fill in the blank" by adding an asterisk (*) in the Google search box at the part of the sentence or phrase that you are unsure of.

Another way to isolate very specific phrases as search terms is to use the plus symbol (+). This tells Google to search for a term only when it appears exactly as you typed it. Say you are looking for information on health care in the United States. You may want to look for only instances of "healthcare" (one word), rather than "health care" (which would yield thousands of sites that mention "health," "care," and "health care." To avoid an abundance of irrelevant results, you would type the following into the search field: +healthcare. Remember not to leave a space after the plus symbol (+).

More with Less: Excluding Terms

There is an even better way to narrow down search results and weed out irrelevant Web sites. Rather than the plus symbol (+), you can use the universal symbol of exclusion or deletion: the minus sign (-). Just as with the plus sign (+), remember that there should be no spaces after the minus sign (-), and you should leave a space before it. That way, Google won't think that you are using a term with a hyphen, such as "T-shirt."

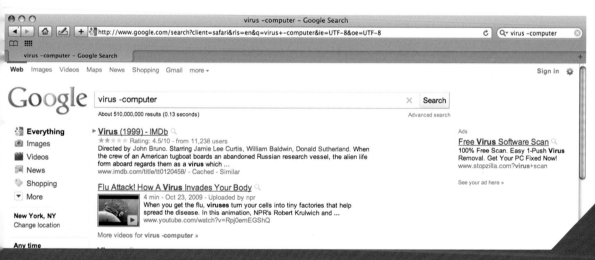

This Google screenshot demonstrates how to perform a search for a common term, like "virus," while still excluding particular criteria to narrow down your search. By excluding "computer," the searcher receives results only on disease-related, rather than computer-related, viruses.

If you were looking for information on disease-causing viruses, but didn't want Google returning any results on computer viruses, you could type in: "virus -computer." This way, you would eliminate all computer virus–related results.

Seeking Synonyms

The tilde (~) is another helpful search symbol. Found on the upper left-hand side of the keyboard, it instructs Google to search for synonyms of the search term or words related to it. Thus, "~ape" yields results for apes, gorillas, and chimpanzees.

One OR the Other

Yet another operator that can help you in your search is the word "OR." Written with both letters capitalized, you can place it between two terms if you want to view results regarding either or both search terms. Maybe you

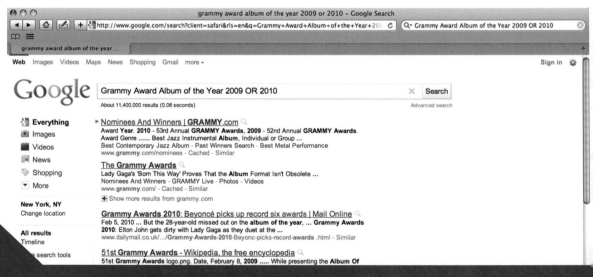

Google's OR operator is a powerful tool that lets you search for one or more terms together. The return results relate to Album of the Year Grammy Awards for 2009 or 2010, or both.

would like to find out who won the Grammy Award for Album of the Year for 2009 or 2010, or both. To find this information, plug in "Grammy Award Album of the Year 2009 OR 2010." Putting in both terms will limit your results to just those pages that mention the Album of the Year Award winner for both those years, rather than all the Album of the Year Award winners throughout the history of the Grammy's.

Ignoring Stop Words

Words like "a," "the," "that," and "an" modify the noun or subject before which they appear. In many cases, Google may ignore them. If you Google "a cat," for example, Google is really looking for the term "cat" and is probably ignoring the "a." In the language of search engines, these are sometimes known as "stop words."

Chapter 2

Getting Advanced with Google

As you deepen your knowledge of Google's capabilities, you will discover that the engine's search methods can be both sharpened and strengthened by the use of certain keywords and the setting of specific parameters. These keywords and parameters tell Google exactly what you're looking for, where you want to search for it, and what kinds of information you want to retrieve and in what format. Knowing how to use these search commands helps generate highly focused, relevant, and useful results.

Narrowing Search Terms and Using Related Searches

Imagine you are working on a report concerning life in France during the Middle Ages. Your search results will, of course, vary according to the search terms you use. The results you will receive by typing "France" into the search box will mostly center upon modern-day France or articles discussing the entire history of France. To zero in more closely on the time period you're

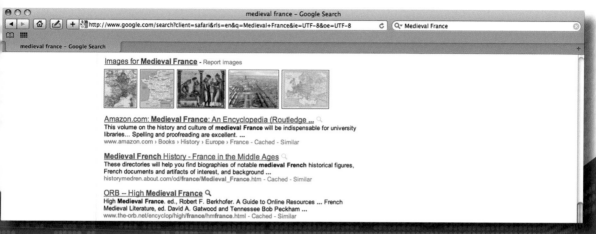

Rather than making your search for France too broad, you can narrow it down with the adjective "medieval" to receive results that apply only to that historical period. You can also hit Google's Image tab to view a wealth of images related to medieval-era France.

interested in, use a search term like "medieval France" or, even more specifically, "fourteenth century France." The results that come back will focus only on the time period you're interested in.

Google helps you refine your searches by listing related searches at the bottom of the page. Scroll down to the bottom of page 1 of your results and you will see "Searches related to medieval france," including links to results for "medieval life france," "medieval paris france," "medieval times france," "medieval castles france," "medieval france religion," "medieval france food," "medieval france map," and other related search terms.

Advanced Search

Just beneath the Search button on Google's main Web search page, you will notice the "Advanced Search" link. This takes you deeper into Google's capabilities. In addition to the normal search field, you will be presented with a large set of criteria that you can select to refine your search.

Advanced Search allows you to tell Google to look for Web pages that contain a certain group of words, an exact wording or phrase, or one or more specific words. You can also tell Google not to show you Web

File   Edit   View   Favorites   Tools   Help

WATCH YOUR LANGUAGE!

Watch Your Language!

You can ask Google to show you only those results written at a certain reading level (excluding results that are for very young readers or for academic experts, for example). You can also request only those Web pages that have been created or modified within the past twenty-four hours, week, month, year, or "anytime." You can even request results that are written in a specific language or originate from a certain country. Perhaps you are fluent in both English and French. Your research could then be conducted in both languages, and Google will present you with results for Web pages written in both English and French.

pages that contain certain unwanted words. For example, let's say you had decided to write on fourteenth-century France. You might now instruct Google to search all Web pages containing the words "medieval France" but ask it to exclude those pages that include the words "thirteenth century France," as they would be beyond the scope of your essay.

One of the more powerful functions in Advanced Search is selecting only those results that are contained within a preferred file type. You are probably familiar with Adobe, Inc.'s Portable Document Format (PDF). A PDF is perhaps the most common type of file for official government documents and publications, scholarly reports, and other content like maps. Other popular formats are Microsoft Word documents (.doc) and other Microsoft Office–generated files, including visual presentations in the PowerPoint format (.ppt) and spreadsheets and lists in Excel format (.xls). You might want to limit your search, for example, to receive only those results that are in a presentation or slideshow format. You would therefore select ".ppt" from the drop-down menu as your desired file type. If you are looking for statistics, budgets, or other "hard data" content, .xls files might be your best bet. Other options include files associated with the Google Earth application, Shockwave files (for animation and other multimedia files), and much more.

The 360-degree camera strapped to this bike rider helped photograph the Royal Palace of Caserta in Caserta, Italy, for the Google Maps museums project.

You can also have Google narrow down things considerably by using the "Search within a site or domain" function within Advanced Search. If you wanted only mentions of a certain search term (for instance, "U.S. military") that appears in articles from the *New York Times* (http://www.nytimes.com), you would plug the *Times'* Web site in the "Search within a site or domain" box. Another method is to select only those results returned from particular types of sites, like those associated with schools, colleges, and universities (any domain names that end in ".edu"). Picking only those sites ending in ".gov" limits your search to official federal and state government Web sites in the United States. If you are working on a multimedia project and need a video component, you can even limit your Google results to a site like YouTube, ensuring that you will only receive video results, rather than text-based ones.

Other features of Advanced Search include numeric ranges indicated by two periods (exs.: 1942..1945; $25,000.. $50,000), requests for where your keyword should appear in a Web page (in the title, the body text, in the URL), and usage rights (whether or not the information on the Web page is free to use, share, or modify).

Putting It All Together

Any one search criterion (keyword, unwanted words, numeric range, file type, reading level, language, etc.) can be very useful. But you can achieve the best, most efficient, and most relevant results by using several search criteria in combination. To test how all these criteria might work together, you can use the example of the 2011 earthquake, tsunami, and nuclear crises in Japan. Say you wanted to find the latest news on the Fukushima I nuclear reactor. You could enter "Fukushima 1" in the search field. Under Advanced Search, you might enter extra words such as "meltdown," "radiation," "deaths," etc.

In addition, you could set the dates to return only hits from the last couple of weeks so that you receive only the most current information. You might set your search criteria to explore resources such as the U.S. Department of State (by selecting ".gov" as the domain). If you want only official U.S. government documents analyzing the crisis, you can select

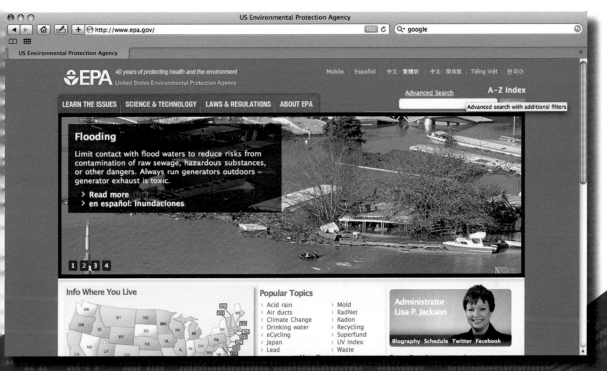

Google and other search engines allow you to creatively drill down to find valuable information from official sites, such as this page on flooding by the U.S. Environmental Protection Agency (http://www.epa.gov).

".gov" as the domain and ".pdf" as the file type. If you happen to be studying Japanese, you may be able to perform some basic research in that language. So you could set the Advanced Search controls to receive Japanese-language results at a basic reading level. If you want audio and video related to the crises in Japan, you might type National Public Radio (http://www.npr.org) and the Public Broadcasting System (http://www. pbs.org) or YouTube into the "Search within a site or domain" box.

As you can see, Google's search capabilities have few limits other than those of your imagination. Play around and experiment with Advanced Search and see how many great information sources across all media you can receive with increasingly narrow and specific search parameters. Google makes research not only easy, but fun!

Chapter 3

Google It: From Start to Finish

Now that we have covered some of the basics, let's examine how to use Google's rich functionality to create, improve, and present a school project. Building on the techniques learned earlier, you will utilize some of Google's other useful functions, such as Google News, Google Maps, and Google Earth, to broaden and enrich your research.

Using Google for a Report on Endangered Species

Let's imagine that you are learning about endangered animal species and you have a research assignment to figure out which nations in the world have done the best job in preserving threatened animals. You need information on what species are endangered in what countries, what role the relevant governments are playing, how zoos and conservation groups are helping, and where there are some important nature preserves.

If you brainstorm a little bit, you can figure out some search terms ("endangered species successful programs"), come up with relevant organizations (World Wildlife Fund), and identify the endangered species and regions you wish to focus on.

At the same time, you can begin to think about how you want to present the information you collect—as a regular research paper or perhaps as a multimedia presentation, with data-rich spreadsheets, charts, photographs, maps, and audio and video components. Google can help you compile all of these different types of information and present them in a single cohesive and compelling presentation.

Starting Your Search

Let's say you begin by simply Googling "Most Endangered Species." On the first results page, you come across an article describing the world's top ten most endangered animals, with the tiger near the top of the list. Within that same article, you pick up some ideas for further searches. It mentions, for example, conservation efforts by the World Wildlife Fund (WWF) and the U.S. Fish & Wildlife Service (FWS) and discusses the nations that are taking the lead in protecting the endangered tigers.

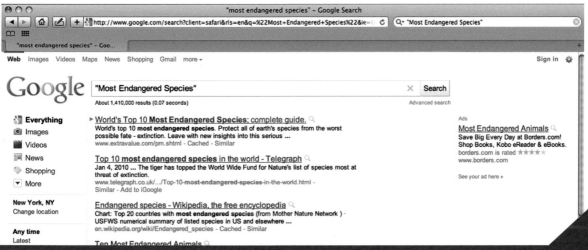

A Google search for "Most Endangered Species" yields research sources as varied as a Wikipedia entry, an article from London's *Telegraph* newspaper, and books related to the topic, among millions of other results.

Expanding Your Parameters

Armed with these new sources of information to investigate, let's revisit Google's Advanced Search. You can do a few different searches for official documents regarding tiger protection efforts on various domains. In the "Search within a site or domain" box, enter the Web site for WWF, FWS, or another conservation organizations, like the Sierra Club or the Natural Resources Defense Council. If you want only government documents and research, enter ".gov" in the domain box. Or, if you only want research provided by nongovernmental conservation organizations, enter ".org" instead. Plug in search terms such as "report," "studies," "findings," or similar words, along with "tiger" and "conservation," to get the latest research from these various groups.

Try narrowing down the search to PDFs. This way, you can restrict your results to official reports and published research on conservation by government agencies and/or nongovernmental organizations. Another possible information stream may be pursued by searching the domains of some of the more prominent zoos, such as the San Diego Zoo and Bronx Zoo.

Web, Images, Videos, Maps, News...and Much More

Searching the Web for pages relevant to your search terms is Google's primary utility. Yet it also offers other search capabilities and Internet utilities. When you go to Google's home page, the "Web" is the natural default setting. This means that when you type a search term into the box, Google will scan the Web for matches. Yet alongside the "Web" setting are several other settings: Images, Videos, Maps, News, Shopping, Gmail, and "More" (Translate, Books, Finance, Scholar, Blogs, Realtime, YouTube, Calendar, Photos, Documents, Reader, Sites, and Groups).

Just as the Web setting retrieves thousands of relevant Web pages based upon your keyword search, the Image tab (used, say, by plugging in "tigers," or "tigers" and "endangered") retrieves thousands of tiger-relevant images. It's another way of searching for information and finding resources you can use in a report. Hence, you might stumble upon information you

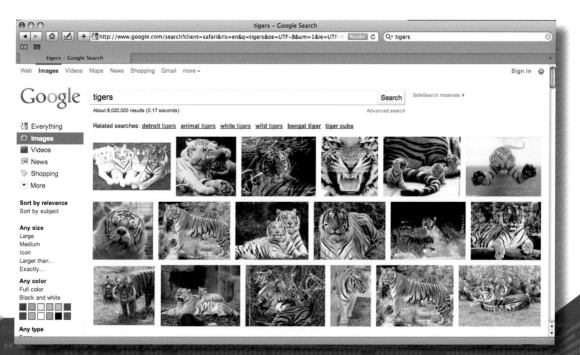

A Google Images search for tigers yields more than eight million results. Public domain images found in such a search can be used in reports and multimedia presentations.

may have overlooked otherwise. Remember, most images are not in the public domain, so you may need permission to use them, even for a school project. So be sure to read all the information a Web site posts regarding image usage before downloading it to your computer or printing it out and using it in a report or presentation. Some Web sites specialize only in public domain images, though they may not have exactly what you're looking for.

Another great source of information for multimedia presentations is Google Maps. For example, you might plug in your ZIP code and find out where the nearest zoos, museums, or other conservation-related institutions are. Visiting these locations to collect materials or interview conservationists, zoologists, or wildlife biologists can be an amazing experience and yield information that will really set your project apart. You can even use Google Maps to find out exactly how to get to these destinations from your home or school.

File   Edit   View   Favorites   Tools   Help

THINK GLOBALLY, SEARCH LOCALLY

Think Globally, Search Locally

One helpful tip when using Google is utilizing ZIP codes to maximize one's searches. Typing in your ZIP code gives the search engine the invaluable clue that it should look for locations matching your query in the immediate vicinity of that ZIP code.

If you plug in the ZIP code of your home or school, you can narrow down your searches of local libraries, museums, community centers, bookstores, restaurants, or any other destinations. You can also use ZIP codes as shortcuts in Google Maps. Plugging in two neighborhoods' ZIP codes will yield the various ways to get from one destination to the other by foot, public transportation, or car, without having to plug in whole addresses.

You can use Google Earth, a powerful version of Google Maps that uses satellite imagery, to check out the terrain and natural habitats of the tiger. You can even zoom into a piece of land, sometimes as small as 100 square yards (84 square meters), and see it in sharp detail. Using Google Earth, you could zoom in on reserves and national parks that provide protected habitat for tigers and use these images in a presentation.

Google News, Google Video, and Other Google Features

One of the most powerful tools in your toolkit is Google's News tab. Keeping the same search terms ("tiger," "conservation," "endangered," etc.), click on News and you will see the latest articles on your topic. As with regular Web searches, you can narrow down your News searches to specific dates. If you only want to know about conservation efforts that have taken place in the most recent calendar year, you can enter that year in your search terms or use the

Seneca Ridge Middle School science instructor Rick Peck uses Google Earth to teach his students about the local watersheds near their school in Sterling, Virginia.

Advanced Search to create a specific date range. You can explore the most recent news or sift through archived articles from many years ago. You can sort your results by date or by relevance.

To really get the best results, you might want to concentrate on news from reputable sources most appropriate to your subject. In this case, we would look to the Web sites of reputable print publications such as *Nature* and *National Geographic*. These Web sites can be entered into the "News Source" box of Google News' Advanced Search page. If there is a certain leading expert on tiger conservation, you can enter his or her name into the "Author" box, and Google will return only those results in which that person was the author. You can also seek news results only from specific countries. This would be useful if you were interested in focusing on India's efforts to protect the Bengal tiger, for example.

File   Edit   View   Favorites   Tools   Help

GOOGLE AT YOUR SERVICE

Google at Your Service

Other useful Google features include Translate (translates documents into the language of your choice), Books (a massive, searchable index of the world's books), Finance (links to the top finance news stories and information on stock quotes, portfolios, and economic trends), Scholar (searches for academic and journal articles and legal opinions), Blogs (presents the leading news stories as discussed on blogs and searches blogs for inputted keywords), Realtime (up-to-the-second social updates, news articles, and blog posts about hot topics), Reader (collects and presents new content from your favorite news sites and blogs), and many, many others.

Using Google's Video search feature, you will find numerous clips about tiger conservation, including ones from video sharing networks like YouTube or Veoh, plus broadcasts from news channels. You can embed these videos into your presentation or simply include links to them.

Google Docs

One of the most powerful and useful of Google's features is Google Docs. This is a suite of online applications hosted by Google that allow you to create documents, presentations, and spreadsheets, along with other multimedia—all for free. Plus, if you have Microsoft Office, Open Office, or other programs, you can upload files created in them to Google Docs, too. All you need to do is sign up for a free Google account, and you can start right away.

Let's say you've done all your research on tiger conservation and are ready to submit your results. You can work entirely online without having to

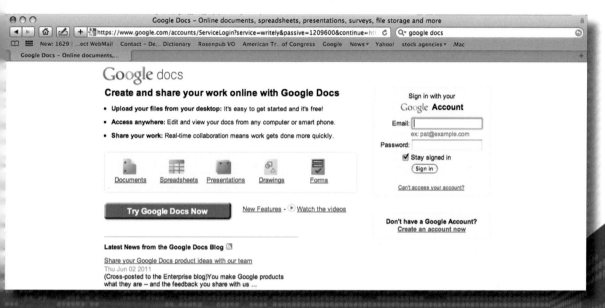

Google Docs allow users to upload their files from their desktop. They can also edit and view their documents, including text files, spreadsheets, presentations, drawings, and forms, from any computer or smartphone.

save your work on a hard drive (although you should always back up your files). Text documents, spreadsheets, graphic organizers, survey and results forms, questionnaires, and entire multimedia presentations that combine text, images, audio, and video can all be created, stored, shared, and presented through Google Docs.

During group projects, you can collaborate with other students on the various aspects of the presentation. Teachers and students alike can access the work in progress, all without having to send attachments back and forth via e-mail or schedule and arrange lots of in-person meetings. With the help of Google Sites, you can even set up a Web site to present your findings, post your report, share your multimedia presentation, and control who can view and/or edit it.

MYTHS & FACTS

MYTH Google is the only search engine.

FACT Google is one of several search engines, but it carries more than 60 percent of the search engine traffic in the United States. Its nearest competitor, Yahoo!, is a distant second, handling about 17 percent of searches requested by American users.

MYTH If you post but then delete your personal information or comments on Web sites and blogs you've accessed via a search engine, they are erased and disappear forever.

FACT You can never be sure how long, and on what servers, your information will continue to exist. Many information technology experts warn that information can remain present and accessible in cyberspace forever.

MYTH The best and most accurate information usually appears on the first page of Google's search results.

FACT You might have to dig deeper and click through numerous pages of results before you find the best information or something that is relevant and useful for your purposes.

Chapter 4

Safe Surfing, Safe Searching

oogle is a powerful gateway to the Internet, and it offers almost infinite possibilities for learning and exploring. But with this enormous new freedom and possibility comes great responsibility—and some very real dangers. Just as you need street smarts offline, you need surf smarts online. In this chapter, we will discuss ways to keep your surfing experiences safe and how to always be a responsible, courteous, and productive, rather than destructive, citizen of the Web.

Your Google Footprint: Be Careful What You Post

We have discussed using Google and its various features and utilities for schoolwork. Of course, much of the time spent on Google is devoted to other pursuits: looking up things we are curious about, checking out viral videos, reading celebrity gossip, looking for addresses, shopping, and much more.

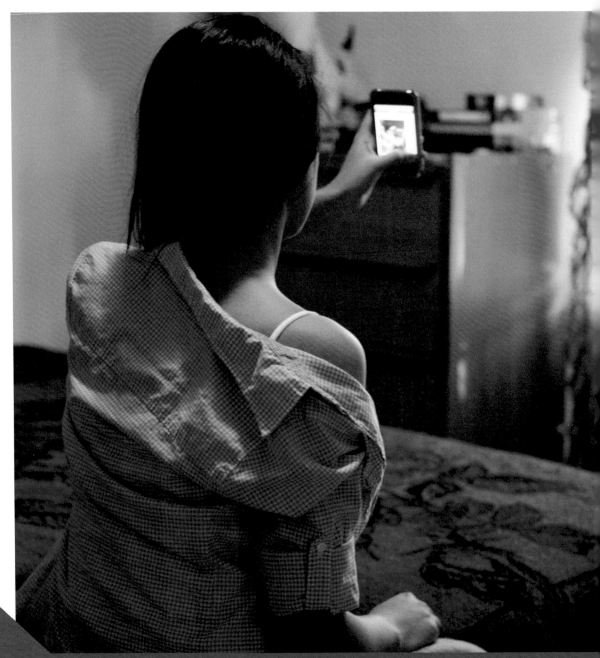

Be careful what you share via the Internet, including photos that are too personal or private. You can never guarantee that the other person will simply keep it to himself or herself and not forward it to dozens or even hundreds of other people.

Just as you can seemingly find information on anything and anyone, remember that the reverse also applies: anyone can find some kind of information on you. Many social networks, even those with secure privacy settings, are searchable, one way or another. If your name appears in a newspaper, on a school-related Web site, in the title of a YouTube video, or in someone's blog or Facebook post, the record is out there in cyberspace forever.

These days, many potential employers Google the name of nearly everyone who applies for a job. Often these Google searches will lead them to Facebook, MySpace, and other social networking sites. You have to be careful about what kind of photos and text you post. This goes for blogs as well. Self-expression is a wonderful and liberating thing, but on the Web, you can't control who will or will not have access to your blog. So when writing a blog post and uploading images to it, consider that people other than your friends and family will be viewing it.

"Don't Be Evil"

Posts to blogs and social networks, all of which can be accessed via Google and other search engines, should never be a forum for attacking, harassing, or bullying other people. Not only is this just plain wrong and a violation of the spirit and ethics of Internet communication, but any hateful or hurtful words will linger forever in cyberspace. They will come back to haunt you. Never write anything online about a person that you would not say to him or her face-to-face. Any disagreements you have with a person should be settled offline and in private, not in a public forum like the Internet.

In the end, it is wise to follow Google's own unofficial motto: "Don't Be Evil." Anything that you consider to be harmful or hurtful in your everyday, offline life is even more so online, where billions of people can be witness to improper and destructive activity. Because much of your online activity can be tracked, you should always be careful not to do anything that is illegal or violates the "community standards" that you agree to when you use any Internet service.

File   Edit   View   Favorites   Tools   Help

EVERYDAY ESSENTIALS

Everyday Essentials

There is a section of Google called "Everyday Essentials," comprised of various features that offer everyday utility. They include:

- Weather: To see the weather for many U.S. and worldwide cities, type "weather" followed by the city and state, U.S. ZIP code, or city and country.
- Stock quotes: To see current market data for a given company or fund, type the ticker symbol into the search box. On the results page, you can click the link to see more data from Google Finance.
- Time: To see the time in many cities around the world, type in "time" and the name of the city.
- Sports Scores: To see scores and schedules for sports teams, type the team name or league name into the search box. This is enabled for many leagues, including the National Basketball Association, National Football League, National Hockey League, and Major League Baseball.
- Sunrise and Sunset: To see the precise times of sunrise and sunset for many U.S. and worldwide cities, type "sunrise" or "sunset" followed by the city name.
- Calculator: To use Google's built-in calculator function, simply enter the calculation you'd like performed into the search box.

Cyberbullying

Entering the vast, virtual world of the Web through Google and other search engines exposes you to many of the same dangers you may face in real life. One of these dangers is bullying. When someone harasses someone else via the Internet, it is known as cyberbullying, and it is an ever-increasing

- □ X

- Books Search: If you're looking for results from a Google Books search, you can enter the name of the author or book title into the search box. Then click on "Books" from the left-hand navigation to view book content. You can click on the record to view more detailed info about that author or title.
- Unit Conversion: You can use Google to convert between many different units of measurement of height, weight, and volume, among many others. Just enter your desired conversion into the search box, and it'll do the rest.
- Local Search: If you're looking for a store, restaurant, or other local business, you can search for the category of business and the location and Google will return results right on the page, along with a map, reviews, and contact information.
- Movie Showtimes: To find reviews and showtimes for movies playing near you, type "movies" or the name of a current film into the Google search box.
- Currency Conversion: To use Google's built-in currency converter, simply enter the conversion you'd like performed into the search box, and it'll provide your answer directly on the results page.
- Maps: Type in the name or U.S. ZIP code of a location and the word "map," and Google will return a map of that location. Clicking on the map will take you to a larger version on Google Maps.

problem. Cyberbullying is the use of digital technologies to express deliberate, repeated, and hostile behaviors toward others. It can happen through e-mail, text messages, instant messages, blogs, or chat rooms in a private or a public format. Social networking sites such as Facebook, Twitter, and MySpace have become places where bullying occasionally occurs among students and other young people.

Tina Meier shows two pictures of her daughter Megan, who committed suicide after allegedly being cyberbullied by a classmate's mother.

A lot of young people are afraid to admit and report that they are being harassed. They may feel that their problems will get worse if they tell someone and draw attention to the situation. Sometimes they are embarrassed that they are being targeted. But the best way to stop a problem is to do something about it. Do not continue to talk to the bully, neither in person nor via electronic communication. It is important to involve a trusted adult.

Even minor cases of cyberbullying can affect a person's well-being, making it difficult to go online, concentrate, or even study or do homework. Severe cases of cyberbullying have led to criminal attacks, and in several cases, it has even led to the suicide of the bullying victim.

Internet Predators

Another very real danger is strangers online who are searching for victims. An Internet predator is someone who uses e-mail, dating sites, online classifieds, social networking sites, and Web portals to make contact with people for the purpose of harming them. A predator may want to rob, deceive, abduct, or attack a person physically or sexually.

Whether they are sexual predators, cyberstalkers, or thieves running an Internet scam, one must always be careful. Remember never to respond to unsolicited or unwanted invitations to chat or communicate in other ways, especially from strangers. Never make plans to meet strangers, no matter how friendly or nice they seem. From the safe invisibility of the keyboard, Internet predators often present themselves as someone your own age or as someone who is a friend of a friend of yours. They may even impersonate someone you know and trust. You must always remain vigilant when communicating on the Internet and not be taken in by predators and imposters. If you are in doubt, or suspect that someone is an Internet predator, do not hesitate to report that person to a family member, teacher, law enforcement officer, or other authority figure, including a Web master or administrator.

Cyberspace can be a very dangerous place. You must always remain vigilant and do all you can to protect yourself against hackers, identity thieves, bullies, stalkers, and other types of Internet predators.

Living Online . . . and Offline

Ultimately, Google is a means to an end: finding the information we need to enrich our lives, whether at school, at home, at work, or at play. Google and other search engines provide a portal to the Internet, through which we can explore an almost infinite number of pathways. We can look up blogs and Web sites devoted to our interests. We can treat Google as a one-stop quick reference guide. It can be used to quickly settle disputes about pop culture trivia, look up movie times, double-check the address of a restaurant, or read a brief biography of a favorite author, musician, or celebrity. We can use Google to compile new content from our favorite blogs and news, sports, and entertainment sites. We can satisfy our curiosity about a new subject of interest, visit forums in which we can share our thoughts and

Ramon Cruz, a student at Burncoat Senior High School in Worchester, Massachusetts, studies in the school library. Going offline to study, research, socialize, and seek entertainment lets you experience a more enriching range of knowledge and experience. Don't just rely on cold virtual reality. Get out into the real world and live life to the fullest.

interact with those who share our interests, or check out sites where we can seek entertainment through music or videos. We can even use Google to access and view our favorite television shows.

However, many people have found that the best kind of life is a balanced one. Spending time online is fine, but it can become a problem if you spend too much of your time doing so. If you are going to school for half of your day, but blogging, chatting online, gaming, and performing Internet search after Internet search for the remainder of your day, you should cut down on your Internet time. Your life is out of balance, and your physical, emotional, and mental health will suffer. Other, non-virtual activities—after-school jobs, sports and physical activity, artistic pursuits, clubs, volunteering, or simply going to hang out with friends or spending time with family and relatives—are enriching, too, and are part of a balanced, healthy life.

Furthermore, doing all of your school assignments online is not the only option available. There is a great deal of knowledge out there that still only resides in books, periodicals, museums, government record archives, and other destinations. While one of Google, Inc.'s aims is to make digital copies of every book ever published available online, it is a goal whose realization is still far off in the future. Logging off and going out into the real world will not only help you live a more balanced life. It will also expose you to a vast realm of knowledge and activities that lie beyond—and inaccessible to—even the most powerful of Internet search engines.

TEN GREAT QUESTIONS

TO ASK AN INFORMATION TECHNOLOGY EXPERT

1 How can Google sometimes tell what you might be about to type before you finish doing so?

2 Is Google the best search engine, or just the most popular?

3 How well does Google safeguard its users' privacy?

4 What does Google do to prevent viruses, hacking, and other destructive activities?

5 What legal action can Google take against those who abuse its community standards or terms of service?

6 What are other Google services that might be useful to me for school, recreation, or work?

7 How exactly do search engines find information or data across the Internet?

8 How will Google and other search engines improve or change in the near and distant future?

9 Is there such a thing as being "addicted" to Googling?

10 What is search engine optimization (SEO)?

GLOSSARY

cyberbullying The use of digital technologies to express deliberate, repeated, and hostile behaviors toward others. It can happen through e-mail, text messages, instant messages, blogs, chat rooms, and social networking sites.

keyword A word specified by a user of a search engine to retrieve desired data.

multimedia The combined use of several media, or types of information delivery, such as sound, text, and video.

PDF Short for Portable Document Format, a file format created by Adobe Systems and used for representing documents in a manner independent of application software, hardware, and operating systems. Each PDF file encapsulates a complete description of a fixed-layout flat document, including the text, fonts, graphics, and other information needed to display it.

search engine A program that finds data or documents on the Internet based on keywords and other search criteria provided by a user.

search engine optimization (SEO) The process by which Web site owners increase the visibility of their Web sites during Internet searches in an attempt to make their Web sites appear near the top of a search's results list.

Shockwave A multimedia software platform that adds animation and interactivity to Web sites.

spreadsheet A common type of electronic document that displays calculations, but can also be used for lists and other functions.

Web server The hardware (and sometimes the software used with it) that makes Internet content accessible.

FOR MORE INFORMATION

Canada Science & Technology Museum
1867 St. Laurent Boulevard
Ottawa, ON K1G 5A3
Canada
(866) 442-4416
Web site: http://www.sciencetech.technomuses.ca
This museum explores the connections among science, technology, and
    changes in Canadian society.

Canadian Internet Project (CIP)
Ryerson University
School of Radio and Television Arts
Toronto, ON M5B 2K3
Canada
(416) 979-5000, ext.7549
Web site: http://www.canadianinternetproject.ca
The Canadian Internet Project is a Ryerson University—based, long-running
    research project centering on Internet usage, trends, attitudes, and
    many other factors in our relationship with the Web.

Computer History Museum
1401 North Shoreline Boulevard
Mountain View, CA 94043
(650) 810-1010
Web site: http://www.computerhistory.org
The Computer History Museum is dedicated to exploring the development of
    computer technology from the twentieth century through to the Internet
    age and beyond.

Family Online Safety Institute (FOSI)
815 Connecticut Avenue, Suite 220
Washington, DC 20006
(202) 572-6252
Web site: http://www.fosi.org
The Family Online Safety Institute is an international, nonprofit organization
that works to develop a safer Internet for children and families. It works
to influence public policies and educate the public.

Get Net Wise
Internet Education Foundation
1634 I Street NW
Washington, DC 20009
Web site: http://www.getnetwise.org
Get Net Wise is part of the Internet Education Foundation, which works to
provide a safe online environment for children and families.

International Technology and Engineering Educators Association (ITEEA)
1914 Association Drive, Suite 201
Reston, VA 20191-1539
(703) 860-2100
Web site: http://www.iteaconnect.org
The International Technology and Engineering Educators Association pro-
motes technology education and literacy.

Internet Keep Safe Coalition
1401 K Street NW, Suite 600
Washington, DC 20005
(866) 794-7233
Web site: http://www.ikeepsafe.org
The Internet Keep Safe Coalition educates children and families about
Internet safety and ethics associated with Internet technologies.

The Internet Society (ISOC)
1775 Wiehle Avenue, Suite 201
Reston, VA 20190-5108
(703) 439-2120
Web site: http://www.isoc.org
The ISOC is a nonprofit organization that concentrates on maintaining high
    standards for Internet infrastructure and promotes education and govern-
    ment policies that promote open online environments.

i-SAFE Inc.
5900 Pasteur Court, Suite #100
Carlsbad, CA 92008
(760) 603-7911
Web site: http://www.isafe.org
Founded in 1998, i-SAFE Inc., is the leader in Internet safety education.
    Available in all fifty states, Washington, D.C., and Department of
    Defense schools across the world, i-SAFE is a nonprofit foundation
    whose mission is to educate and empower youth to make their Internet
    experiences safe and responsible. The goal is to educate students on
    how to avoid dangerous, inappropriate, or unlawful online behavior.

Media Awareness Network
1500 Merivale Road, 3rd Floor
Ottawa, ON K2E 6Z5
Canada
(613) 224-7721
Web site: http://www.media-awareness.ca
The Media Awareness Network creates media literacy programs for young
    people. The site contains educational games about the Internet and media.

NetSmartz
Charles B. Wang International Children's Building

699 Prince Street
Alexandria, VA 22314-3175
(800) 843-5678
Web site: http://www.netsmartz.org
NetSmartz provides children, teens, and parents with resources on how to
    surf the Internet safely.

World Wide Web Consortium (W3C)
32 Vassar Street, Room 32-G515
Cambridge, MA 02139
Web site: http://www.w3.org
The W3C is the main international body that brings together many players to
    help set standards, technological and otherwise, for the Internet.

Web Sites

Due to the changing nature of Internet links, Rosen Publishing has developed
an online list of Web sites related to the subject of this book. This site is
updated regularly. Please use this link to access the list:

http://www.rosenlinks.com/dil/goog

FOR FURTHER READING

Brasch, Nicolas. *The Internet* (Technology Behind). Mankato, MN: Smart Apple Media, 2011.

Bullard, Lisa. *Ace Your Oral or Multimedia Presentation*. Berkeley Heights, NJ: Enslow Elementary, 2009.

Cindrich, Sharon, and Ali Douglass. *A Smart Girl's Guide to the Internet: How to Connect with Friends, Find What You Need, and Stay Safe Online* (American Girl Library). Middleton, WI: American Girl Publishing, 2009.

Dougherty, Terri. *Freedom of Expression and the Internet* (Hot Topics). Farmington Hills, MI: Lucent Books, 2009.

Espejo, Roman. *Does the Internet Increase Crime?* (At Issue). Farmington Hills, MI: Greenhaven Press, 2010.

Furgang, Adam. *Searching Online for Image, Audio, and Video Files* (Digital and Information Literacy). New York, NY: Rosen Publishing, 2009.

Gaines, Ann Graham. *Ace Your Internet Research* (Ace It! Information Literacy). Berkeley Heights, NJ: Enslow Publishers, 2009.

Gilbert, Sara. *Built for Success: The Story of Google*. Mankato, MN: Creative Paperbacks, 2011.

Hamen, Susan E. *Google: The Company and Its Founders* (Technology Pioneers). North Mankato, MN: Essential Library, 2011.

Shaw, Maura D. *Mastering Online Research*. Cincinnati, OH: Writer's Digest Books, 2007.

Stewart, Gail B. *Larry Page and Sergey Brin: The Google Guys* (Innovators). Farmington Hills, MI: Kidhaven Press, 2007.

Willard, Nancy E. *Cyber-Safe Kids, Cyber-Savvy Teens: Helping Young People Learn to Use the Internet Safely and Responsibly*. San Francisco, CA: Jossey-Bass, 2007.

BIBLIOGRAPHY

Dornfest, Rael, Paul Bausch, and Tara Calishain. *Google Hacks: Tips and Tools for Finding and Using the World's Information*. Sebastopol, CA: O'Reilly Media, 2006.

Gaudin, Sharon. "Google, Facebook Battle for 'Future of the Web.'" *PC World*, October 14, 2010. Retrieved March 2011 (http://www.pcworld.com/article/207916/ google_facebook_battle_for_future_of_the_web.html).

Google.com. "Google Basic Search Help." Retrieved March 2011 (http://www.google.com/help/customize.html).

Google.com. "Google Search Basics." Retrieved March 2011 (http://www.google.com/support/websearch/bin/topic.py?topic=351).

Google.com. "Teaching Using Google Earth." Retrieved March 2011 (http://sitescontent.google.com/google-earth-for-educators).

Husted, Bill. "Virus Makers Taking New Route to Your PC." *Atlanta Journal-Constitution*, April 26, 2011. Retrieved April 2011 (http://www.ajc.com/lifestyle/virus-makers-taking-new-925547.html?cxtype=rss_news_128746).

Levy, Steven. *In the Plex: How Google Thinks, Works, and Shapes Our Lives*. New York, NY: Simon & Schuster, 2011.

McCracken, Harry. "Google's War Against Rotten Search Results." *Time*, March 3, 2001. Retrieved April 2011 (http://www.time.com/time/business/article/0,8599,2056576,00.html).

Merrill, Douglas C., and James A. Martin. *Getting Organized in the Google Era: How to Stay Efficient, Productive (and Sane) in an Information-Saturated World*. New York, NY: Crown Business, 2011.

Miller, Michael. *Googlepedia: The Ultimate Google Resource*. 3rd ed. Upper Saddle River, NJ: Que, 2008.

The New Atlantis, eds. "Gaga Over Google." *The New Atlantis*,
    2004. Retrieved March 2011 (http://www.thenewatlantis.com/
    publications/gaga-over-google).

Stross, Randall E. *Planet Google: One Company's Audacious Plan to
    Organize Everything We Know*. New York, NY: Free Press, 2009.

University of North Carolina-Asheville. "Information for Literacy Instruction."
    Retrieved March 2011 (http://www.lib.unca.edu/library/infolit/
    google_research.html).

Vise, David A., and Mark Malseed. *The Google Story: Inside the Hottest
    Business, Media, and Technology Success of Our Time*. New York,
    NY: Delacorte Press, 2005.

Weinberg, Tamar. "Generation Google: A Talk with Today's Teens." Search
    Engine Roundtable, February 28, 2008. Retrieved March 2011
    (http://www.seroundtable.com/archives/016410.html).

Whitney, Lance. "Google's Market Share Dips Ever So Slightly." CNET
    News, September 10, 2010. Retrieved March 2011 (http://news.
    cnet.com/8301-1023_3-20016795-93.html).

YouTube.com. "Google Docs Tour." Retrieved March 2011 (http://www.
    youtube.com/GoogleDocsCommunity).

INDEX

About the Author

Philip Wolny is a writer and editor living in New York. He has written extensively on computers, computer programs, and computer technology, including books on creating, using, and interpreting spreadsheets; creating electronic graphic organizers; and Foursquare and other geosocial network services. Whether researching projects or working on academic books, Wolny scarcely remembers how he managed before Google came along and fondly recalls some of his very first searches in the late 1990s.

Photo Credits

Cover (background) and interior graphics © www.istockphoto.com/suprun; cover and p. 1 (left to right) © www.istockphoto.com/tbradford, © www.istockphoto.com/zhang bo, © www.istockphoto.com/Nikada, © www.istockphoto.com/Trevor Smith; p. 5 Chris Jackson/Getty Images; p. 15 Franco Origlia/Getty Images; p. 23 Tracy A. Woodward/The Washington Post/Getty Images; p. 28 J. Emilio Flores/La Opinion/Newscom; p. 32 © AP Images; p. 34 Shutterstock.com; p. 34 Barry Chin/The Boston Globe via Getty Images.

Designer: Nicole Russo; Photo Researcher: Amy Feinberg